P9-CCB-004

# Over the Steamy Swamp

DISCARD

HBJ

First published 1988 by Hutchinson Children's Books, London
Copyright © 1988 by Paul Geraghty

Requests for permission to make copies of
any part of the work should be mailed to:
Permissions, Harcourt Brace Jovanovich, Publishers,
Orlando, Florida 32887.

Library of Congress Cataloging-in-Publication Data

Geraghty, Paul.
Over the steamy swamp/Paul Geraghty.—1st U.S. ed.
p.   cm.
"Gulliver books."
Summary: A hungry mosquito starts a food chain
in a steamy swamp as each hungry animal
both preys and is preyed upon.
ISBN 0-15-200561-7
1. Food chains (Ecology)—Pictorial works—Juvenile literature.
2. Swamp ecology—Pictorial works—Juvenile literature.
[1. Swamp animals. 2. Swamp ecology.] I. Title.
QH541.14.G47   1989
591.5'26325—dc19          88-21319

Printed in Portugal
First U.S. edition 1989
A B C D E

# Over the Steamy Swamp

## Paul Geraghty

**Gulliver Books**

**Harcourt Brace Jovanovich**

San Diego    New York    London

To the Wasps: Divad Gardinium, Terenzio Fandango
and Marcus Mantis Frérém

One steamy afternoon
a mosquito flew over a swamp.

She was too tired and hungry to notice . . .

. . . a greedy dragonfly watching her.

And the dragonfly was too interested in the mosquito to notice . . .

. . . a famished frog watching him watching the mosquito.

But the frog was so excited she didn't see . . .

... a peckish fish watching her
watching the dragonfly
watching the mosquito.

And the fish was too busy thinking about the frog to notice . . .

. . . a hungry heron watching her
watching the frog
watching the dragonfly
watching the mosquito.

The heron was too busy thinking about dinner to notice . . .

...a starving snake watching him
watching the fish
watching the frog
watching the dragonfly
watching the mosquito.

But the snake was so stealthily slithering she didn't see...

...a craving crocodile watching her
watching the heron
watching the fish
watching the frog
watching the dragonfly
watching the mosquito.

The crocodile was too hungry to look round and see...

. . . a hostile hunter watching him
watching the snake
watching the heron
watching the fish
watching the frog
watching the dragonfly
watching the mosquito.

And the hunter had no idea that . . .

. . . a great, big, ravenous lion was watching him
watching the crocodile
watching the snake
watching the heron
watching the fish
watching the frog
watching the dragonfly
watching the mosquito.

The great, big, ravenous lion was too busy preparing to pounce to notice . . .

. . . the mosquito
that landed on his great, big nose and bit him.

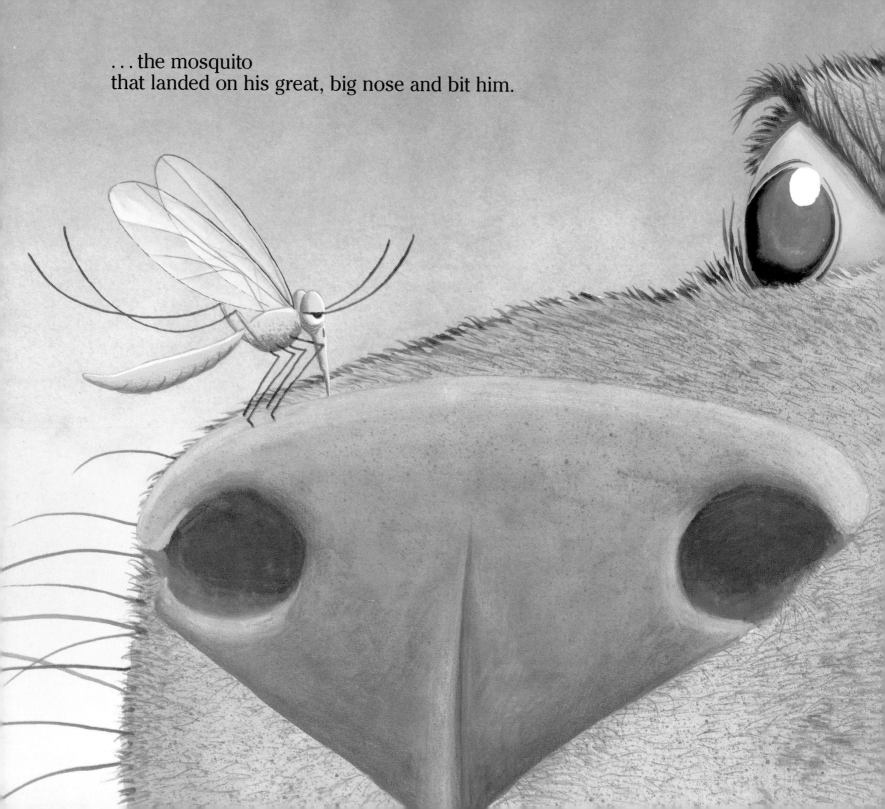

"YEOW!" yelled the lion.

The startled snake
saw the cowering crocodile
seeing the horrified hunter
seeing the great, big, ravenous lion
that yelled, 'YEOW!'

The frightened fish saw the hysterical heron
seeing the startled snake
seeing the cowering crocodile
seeing the horrified hunter
seeing the great, big, ravenous lion that yelled, "YEOW!"

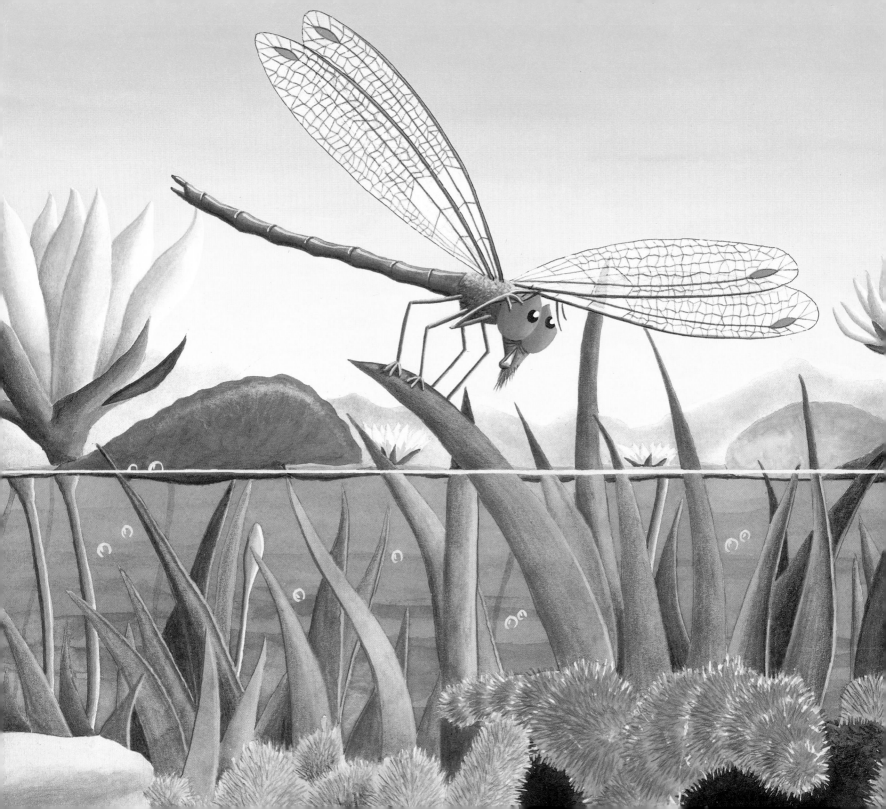

The dismayed dragonfly saw the flabbergasted frog
seeing the frightened fish
seeing the hysterical heron
seeing the startled snake
seeing the cowering crocodile
seeing the horrified hunter
seeing the great, big, ravenous lion that yelled, "YEOW!"

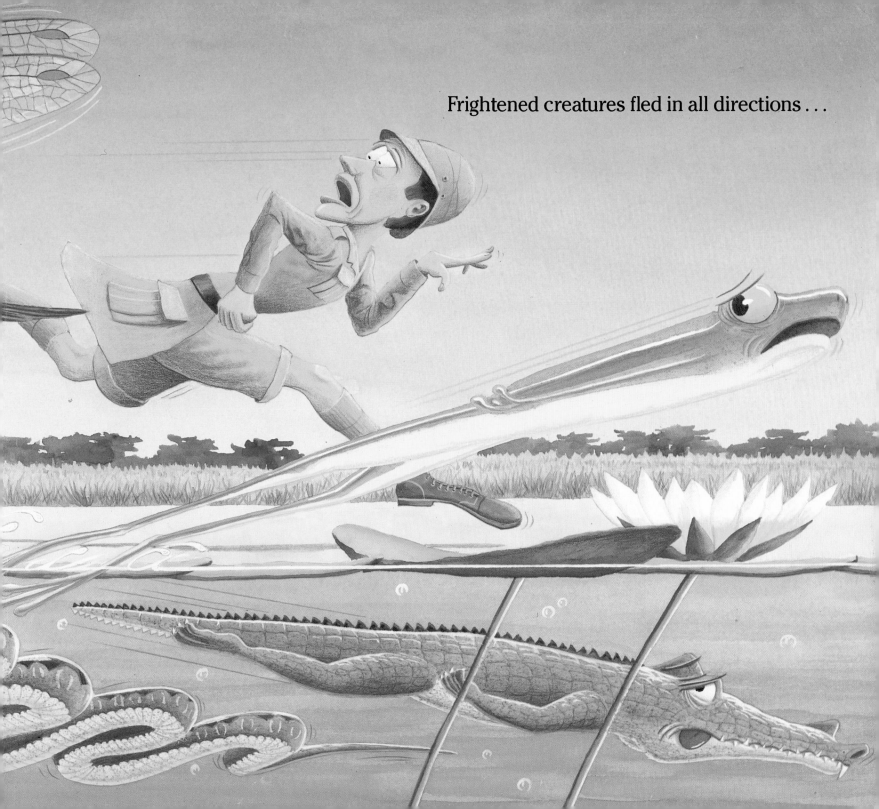

Frightened creatures fled in all directions . . .

... and a fat mosquito flew back over the silent swamp.